LISTENING FOR GOD
THROUGH
PHILIPPIANS

Lectio Divina Bible Studies

wph publishing house
Indianapolis, Indiana

Beacon Hill Press of Kansas City
Kansas City, Missouri

ABOUT THE
LECTIO DIVINA
BIBLE STUDIES

ectio divina, Latin for *divine reading*, is the ancient Christian
practice of communicating with God through the reading and
study of Scripture. Throughout history, great Christian leaders
including John Wesley have used and adapted this ancient
method of interpreting Scripture. This Bible study builds on
this practice, introducing modern readers of the Bible to the
time-honored tradition of "listening for God" through His Word.
In this series, the traditional *lectio divina* model has been revised
and expanded for use in group Bible study. Each session in this
study includes the following elements. (Latin equivalents are
noted in italics.)

- Summary   A brief overview of the session.
  Epitome

- Silence   A time of quieting oneself prior to
  Silencio   reading the Word.

- Preparation   Focusing the mind on the central
  Praeparatio   theme of the text.

- Reading   Carefully reading a passage of
  Lectio   Scripture.

- Meditation   Exploring the meaning of the Bible
  Meditatio   passage.

- Contemplation   Yielding oneself to God's will.
  Contemplatio

- Prayer   Expressing praise, thanksgiving,
  Oratio   confession, or agreement to God.

- Incarnation   Resolving to act on the message of
  Incarnatio   Scripture.

The Lectio Divina Bible Studies invite readers to slow down, read Scripture, meditate upon it, and prayerfully respond to God's Word.

CONTENTS

INTRODUCTION

Among the epistles included in the New Testament canon, Paul's letter to the Philippian church stands out as the kindest and gentlest of them all. Far from the strong, harsh indictments of Galations or the deep theological lessons of Romans, the book of Philippians is filled with statements of rejoicing, prayerful thanksgiving, loving compassion, and gentle exhortation.

The city of Philippi was a thriving Roman colony, and its citizens (mostly Greek, but also including some Romans and Jews) were afforded the highly prized benefit of Roman citizenship. The church at Philippi was founded by the Apostle Paul on his second missionary journey. Its first converts were Lydia, who was a dealer in purple fabric, and members of her household, according Luke's account in Acts 16:13–15. Paul's compassionate prayer for the Philippian believers denotes his personal attachment to and fondness for this family of faith (Philippians 1:3–11).

While many threads run through this four-chapter book, a dominant theme is that Jesus Christ and living the way He directs have a direct impact on everyday life.

Paul wrote this letter from prison. This fact makes all the more powerful the exhortation offered in the fourth chapter: "Do not be anxious about anything, but in everything, by prayer and petition, with thanksgiving, present your requests to God. And the peace of God, which transcends all understanding, will guard your hearts and your minds in Christ Jesus" (Philippians 4:6–7).

NEVER ALONE IN THE JOURNEY

Listening for God through Philippians 1:1–11

Epitome

SUMMARY

O ur walk with God is never a solo act. Although there may be seasons when we feel isolated, we share the road with many sisters and brothers. On many occasions during his ministry, the Apostle Paul would have had the right to feel alone in his walk with Christ. When he was locked in prison or under house arrest, he might easily have imagined that he was by himself.

However, Paul adamantly maintained in his letters that numerous persons were with him and many partners supported him. Some prayed for him, some provided material support, and others carried on the work when he was unable. Whether freely proclaiming the good news or bound in chains, Paul knew that he belonged to a team. He was well aware that others stood with him by providing encouragement and support.

We also are a part of a great team. Our lives are intimately connected with fellow sisters and brothers. Together, we share memories of yesterday and hopes for tomorrow, testify to great victories, and share the heavy loads.

SILENCE ✝ LISTEN FOR GOD

Sit quietly and ponder the fact that you are a part of something much larger than yourself. Listen as God reminds you of other members of His family.

PREPARATION ✝ FOCUS YOUR THOUGHTS

Who have been the two or three most influential people in your life?

In what ways have these people influenced you?

In what ways have they been partners or teammates in your life?

Lectio Reading † Hear the Word

The church at Philippi was one of Paul's great joys. It is not by accident that the word *joy*, in some form, occurs sixteen times in this letter. In Acts 16 we read of Paul's establishment of this church. At Philippi, Lydia opened her heart to the Lord, and Paul and Silas experienced their miraculous escape from prison as they sang praises to God.

In the ensuing years, the cordial relationship between Paul and the Philippian church continued. When the Philippians heard of Paul's imprisonment, they sent a gift to him. In this thank-you letter, Paul expressed his deep gratitude, not for the gift only, but also for the givers themselves.

Instead of including a traditional prayer of thanksgiving, Paul began this letter by describing his recent prayers for the Philippians as prayers of joy. He proceeded then to pray for his Philippian partners. In particular, he prayed that their love would continue to mature.

Paul used several words and phrases of great significance to express his prayer for the Philippians:

Partnership: Active participation.

Day of Christ Jesus: The return of Christ when the work begun by Christ will be brought to its completion.

Fruit of righteousness: Concrete expressions of a right relationship with God.

Read Philippians 1:1–11, paying special attention to how these words and phrases shape the content of Paul's opening message to these beloved people.

MEDITATION ✝ ENGAGE THE WORD

Meditate on Philippians 1:1–8

Paul expressed his gratitude for the Philippians, particularly noting that his prayers were filled with joy due to their partnership in the gospel. What do you think Paul means by *partnership*? What makes a relationship between people a partnership? What other words might be used to describe this kind of relationship?

Read the sidebar quote by Dietrich Bonhoeffer. How is participating in a community different than simply belonging to a community?

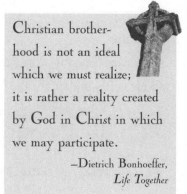

Christian brotherhood is not an ideal which we must realize; it is rather a reality created by God in Christ in which we may participate.

—Dietrich Bonhoeffer,
Life Together

Why would thinking about his partnership with the Philippians bring joy to Paul? What is joy? Given the fact that Paul was in prison while writing this letter, what other circumstance in his life might have accounted for his ability to feel joy at that moment?

Can the Christian life be lived alone? Why or why not?

Read the sidebar quote by Kent Ira Groff. Do you agree with this statement? Why or why not?

> Without the discipline of community, solitude degenerates into self-absorption and isolation.
>
> –Kent Ira Groff, *Journeyman*

With whom in the body of Christ do you share an authentic partnership? What is that partnership like?

Are your partnerships with other Christians important to you? Why or why not? Compare the way you feel about your relationships with other Christians to the way Paul felt about his partnership with the Philippians. What might improve or strengthen your partnership with others believers?

Meditate on Philippians 1:9–11

Since Paul had already acknowledged the love of the Philippians, why would he then pray that their love would abound "more and more in knowledge and depth of insight"?

Describe the difference between the love Paul describes here and sentimental emotions that we usually think of as love.

Read the sidebar quote by Carlo Carretto. How do you respond to what Carretto says concerning love?

> Love will make demands on us. It will question us from within. It will disturb us. Sadden us. Play havoc with our feelings. Harass us. Reveal our superficialities. But at last it will bring us to the light.
> —Carlo Carretto, *Why, O Lord?*

How does Paul's prayer here compare to his prayer in Colossians 1:9–12?

What do you think Paul means by the phrase *pure and blameless*? In what ways have you seen that concept misunderstood by Christians?

Name some examples of "fruit of righteousness."

In what areas of your life are you seeking God's guidance to discern what is best?

Does your life display a complete, undivided loyalty to Christ? In what areas do you struggle to declare complete allegiance to Christ?

What are the greatest challenges you face in bearing fruit of righteousness?

CONTEMPLATION ✝ REFLECT AND YIELD

In what ways have you attempted to make the journey with God a solo trek?

About what areas of your life has God said, "I began the work, and I will complete it"?

In what ways might God be calling you to share the journey with other Christians?

Oratio
PRAYER ✦ RESPOND TO GOD

Who are the partners with whom you share the journey?

How is God calling you to experience this partnership in deeper ways?

Join one other person in praying the prayer by Charles Wesley in the sidebar. Ask God to make you a dependable partner.

Help us to help each other, Lord,

Each other's cross to bear;

Let all their friendly aid afford,

And feel each other's care.

–Charles Wesley, "Jesus, United by Thy Grace"

Incarnatio
INCARNATION ✦ LIVE THE WORD

Name two people to whom you can express gratitude for their partnership with you in the gospel. Communicate your thanks to them within the next seven days.

TRIUMPH THROUGH ADVERSITY

Listening for God through Philippians 1:12–30

SUMMARY

B ad things happen to good people. So the question is not whether bad things will happen but what will result from them.

Paul's life is a testimony to our ability to thrive in spite of difficult circumstances. In 2 Corinthians 11:23–28, Paul recited a long list of adversities he had faced. Yet he did not waste time speculating on the reason these tough times had come his way. He simply acknowledged that they had come. In spite of the difficulties he had faced, Paul remained confident and faithful. He never gave up but continued to run the race of faith. He was convinced that whatever the circumstance, God can transform it into a triumph.

That should be no surprise to followers of Jesus Christ. At the core of our faith is the belief that beyond the cross lies an empty tomb. Darkness is always broken by light; hopelessness always gives way to despair; and even death results in new life.

As a follower of the resurrected Christ, you can discover triumph through adversity.

SILENCE ✝ LISTEN FOR GOD

Quiet yourself in the presence of God and repeat aloud this simple confession: "Christ is risen." Pause to allow the living Christ to enliven you with His presence.

PREPARATION ✝ FOCUS YOUR THOUGHTS

Describe a time when you (or a loved one) experienced hardship. How did you respond to that situation?

List various reactions people have when faced with some difficulty.

Lectio
Reading ✝ Hear the Word

At the time of his writing to the Philippians, Paul was imprisoned, most likely under house arrest in Rome (see Acts 28:14–31).

The congregation at Philippi also was facing adversity. While we are not certain of their specific struggles, we know that some were being persecuted by civil officials. In addition, some teachers who were preaching a message different than that of Paul were infiltrating the church, and there may have been some internal struggles within the church (see Philippians 3:2, 18–19; 4:2). When writing to the Philippians, Paul used his own suffering as a paradigm for dealing with the difficulties they were facing. But Paul didn't make himself out to be a hero. He pointed to the success of the gospel that had resulted from his suffering.

In his encouragement to the people at Philippi, Paul uses the following terms:

Palace guard: This term may refer either to a governor's palace in a Roman province or to a contingent of several thousand soldiers in Rome.

Chains: While Paul may literally have been in chains, the term is a metaphor for his suffering, specifically his imprisonment.

Exalted in my body: The term *exalted* or *lifted up* reminds the readers of Christ being lifted up on the cross.

Live your lives: Literally, *live as citizens,* thus a reminder of their true citizenship.

Contending as one man: Working together as a team.

Read Philippians 1:12–30.

MEDITATION ✝ ENGAGE THE WORD

Meditate on Philippians 1:12–14

Paul told the Philippians that the adversity he had suffered, specifically his imprisonment, had served to promote the gospel. Read the quote by Carlo Carretto in the sidebar. What

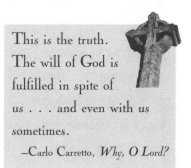

This is the truth. The will of God is fulfilled in spite of us . . . and even with us sometimes.

—Carlo Carretto, *Why, O Lord?*

does this statement imply about the work of God's kingdom?

Paul saw his adversity as a witness to those who were causing his suffering as well as to others in the prison. In what ways would it have been a witness to these persons?

What is there about Paul's adversity that would have pointed to Christ?

Read the sidebar quote by Hermann Bezzel on page 21. How do Christians most often deal with suffering? Why would

Bezzel say that "suffering is the greatest work in the discipleship of Jesus"?

How would Paul's adversity have encouraged fellow Christians to speak the word of God more courageously?

> Suffering is the highest action of Christian obedience; and I call blessed, not those who have worked, but all who have suffered. Suffering is the greatest work in the discipleship of Jesus.
>
> —Hermann Bezzel, quoted in Pastoralblatter

In what ways have you seen fellow Christians remain faithful to God in the midst of difficult situations? What effect has their example had upon you?

Are "chains" for Christ something we decide to take up on our own, or do they come to us? Explain your response.

What "chains" for Christ are you wearing right now?

Meditate on Philippians 1:15–18

What do you think Paul meant when he said that some preach Christ out of envy, rivalry, and selfish ambition? Can you describe a situation in which you have seen the gospel preached in that way? How did you react? How did other Christians react?

Does Paul's response to people who preach the gospel for false motives surprise you? Why or why not?

What lessons about conflict among God's people can you draw from Paul's attitude?

Read the sidebar quote by Stephen V. Doughty. In what ways can conflict among the people of God actually lead to growth?

How do you handle conflict among God's people?

> The more I see of conflict in the church, the more I am moved by persons who allow conflict to become the occasion of their growth. . . . Jesus seeks to form us even in the places of greatest friction. In the midst of division and hurt, He can draw us toward maturity in fresh and formative ways.
>
> —Stephen V. Doughty,
> *Discovering Community*

Do you find it difficult to accept Paul's idea that the most important thing is that Christ is preached, regardless of the motives of those involved? Why or why not?

Meditate on Philippians 1:19–26

Paul was confident that no matter what happened to him, Christ would be exalted in his body. What do you think he meant?

Read the sidebar quote by Simone Weil. Do you agree with this statement? Why or why not?

> Affliction makes God appear to be absent for a time, more absent than a dead man, more absent than light in the utter darkness of a cell. A kind of horror submerges the whole soul.
>
> —Simone Weil, Waiting for God

How might Christ be exalted through suffering and death?

Do you believe that Paul most wanted to continue living and preaching the gospel, or to die and be with Christ? Explain your response.

Could you honestly make the statement that Paul made: "For to me, to live is Christ and to die is gain"? If not, what changes in your thinking would need to occur before you could make such a statement?

Meditate on Philippians 1:27–30

What does a life look like that is "worthy of the gospel of Christ"?

Paraphrase what Paul meant by saying, "You stand firm in one spirit, contending as one man for the faith of the gospel."

Describe a situation in which you saw God's people stand "firm in one spirit, contending as one man" in the midst of adversity. What was the outcome?

Read the sidebar quote by Dom Augustin Guillerand. How do you normally respond when you identify shortcomings or faults in your life? How do you normally handle adversity in your life?

> God will know how to draw glory even from our faults. Not to be downcast after committing a fault is one of the marks of true sanctity.
> —Dom Augustin Guillerand

Do you prefer to work out difficult situations on your own or with the help of others? Why?

CONTEMPLATION ✝ REFLECT AND YIELD

How would your life change if you adopted Paul's attitude that "to live is Christ and to die is gain"?

What would change in your life if you lived every moment in "a manner worthy of the gospel of Christ"?

PRAYER ✝ RESPOND TO GOD

What difficult situation are you now facing? What is your greatest need—courage, faith, endurance, or something else?

In silent prayer, submit your adversities to God and ask, "Lord, how can You be glorified in this situation?"

INCARNATION ✝ LIVE THE WORD

Paul was convinced that in all situations, including adversity, Jesus Christ can be magnified. Resolve to seek God's will and His glory each day this week, no matter how difficult the circumstances may be.

A NEW WAY
OF THINKING

Listening for God through Philippians 2:1–18

SUMMARY

L iving the Christian life is more than amending old habits. More than a reformation of lifestyle, it is a transformation of the mind (Romans 12:1–2). Ultimately, it is our minds that are changed after we come to Christ.

Paul invited the Philippian believers to undergo a change of mind by taking on the thinking of Jesus Christ. That would involve a spiritual death and resurrection.

That invitation would have presented a challenge to the self-centered, accomplishment-driven society in which the Philippians lived. This new way of thinking would call for a lifestyle in which all actions were considered in light of the interests of other people.

Although the Philippian church was a generous congregation, this challenge would have seemed a near impossibility to them. However, Paul's call for them was not merely to try harder to be good but to be transformed into the likeness of Christ through the power of the Holy Spirit.

Like the Philippians, you, too, are surrounded by a self-centered, accomplishment-driven culture. And, like them, God calls you to participate in this alternative way of thinking—to take on the mind of Jesus Christ.

SILENCE ✝ LISTEN FOR GOD

Focus your mind on the self-giving love of Christ, which He demonstrated on the cross. Listen to Him speak words of grace, forgiveness, and love to you.

PREPARATION ✝ FOCUS YOUR THOUGHTS

Describe a time when someone tried to change your mind. What did that person do to try to persuade or change you?

Did it work? Did your thinking really change, or did you continue in your old way of thinking?

Lectio
READING ✝ HEAR THE WORD

Paul admonished the Philippians to live in unity with each other. While we have no indication that there was a significant conflict in that congregation, Paul did request assistance in helping two women, Euodia and Syntyche, to "be of the same mind in the Lord" (Philippians 4:2 KJV). Paul called the Philippians both *communally* and *individually* to participate in the mind of Jesus Christ. In what may have been an early hymn describing Christ's suffering, death, resurrection, and ascension, Paul sets the standard for the Christian worldview. It is the mind of Christ (2:6–11).

Read Philippians 2:1–18, paying particular attention to these key terms in Paul's admonition:

Like-minded: Having one mind—the mind of Christ.

Something to be grasped: Grasped can mean "to hold on to." It can also mean "to exploit" or "to take advantage of."

Made himself nothing: Literally, this phrase means "He emptied himself."

Nature: This word, which can also mean *form*, describes the manner in which Christ was actually God but took on the form of a servant.

Work out your salvation: This phrase does not imply that we are saved by what we do but that we should act upon what we believe.

Drink offering: An Old Testament ritual expressing gratitude.

MEDITATION ✝ ENGAGE THE WORD

Meditate on Philippians 2:1–5

Throughout his letter Paul spoke of the joy the Philippian church brought to him. What could it mean that they would make his joy complete?

Describe what a community of believers would look like if it were "like-minded, having the same love, being one in spirit and purpose." Can like-minded people ever disagree? Explain your answer.

Is there a difference between *uniformity* and *unity*? If so, what is it? To which did Paul call the Philippian Christians?

Describe what a community of believers would look like if it did nothing out of selfish ambition but acted solely on the concerns of others. What prevents individuals from doing this? What prevents congregations from doing this?

In what areas of your life do you observe selfish ambition or conceit?

In what specific relationships of your life is God calling you to look to the interests of others? Do you find that difficult to do? If so, why?

Would it be easier if Paul had written, "Let your actions be the same as Jesus Christ's," rather than, "Your attitude should be the same as that of Christ Jesus"? Why or why not?

Meditate on Philippians 2:6–11

What do you think Paul meant when he said that Jesus made himself "nothing"?

What incidents in the life of Jesus illustrate this self-concept?

In which incidents in Jesus' life might he have been tempted to abandon the role of servant?

Read the sidebar quote by Henri Nouwen, Donald McNeill, and Douglas Morrison. Do you agree with the statement? How does this idea shape your understanding of the nature of God?

What difference does it make that the exaltation of Christ is based upon His humiliation through suffering and death?

What attitudes or opinions that you hold would need to be changed if you were to take on the role of servant?

[Jesus'] becoming a servant is not an exception to His being God. His self-emptying and humiliation are not a step away from His true nature. His becoming as we are and dying on a cross is not a temporary interruption of His own divine existence. Rather, in the emptied and humbled Christ we encounter God, we see who God really is, we come to know His true divinity.

—Henri Nouwen, Donald McNeill, and Douglas Morrison, *Compassion*

If you were to take on the role of servant, how would that affect your relationships?

It has been said that there is no resurrection with crucifixion. If you were to embrace that concept, how would it affect your life?

Meditate on Philippians 2:12–18

As a staunch believer in God's grace, Paul certainly did not promote the idea that we are saved by works—that is, because of the good things we do. Yet he knew that the mindset of Christ must be applied to day-to-day living.

Read the sidebar quote by Teresa of Avila. In Avila's opinion, what is the relationship between belief and action?

> Our works have no value unless they are united with faith, and our faith has no value unless it is united with works.
>
> —Teresa of Avila, *Interior Castle*

In light of Paul's admonition to work out our salvation with fear and trembling, what is the significance of his next statement: "It is God who works in you to will and to act according to his good purpose"?

How would you describe the relationship between *willing* and *acting*?

How will you work out the mind of Christ in your school or workplace? Your home? Your church?

Read the second sidebar quote by Henri Nouwen. Describe the cross you are presently carrying.

> Each of us has a cross to carry. There is no need to make one or look for one. The cross we have is hard enough for us! But are we willing to take it up, to accept it as our cross?
>
> —Henri Nouwen,
> *Bread for the Journey*

How does it affect your walk with God to know that it is He who enables you to both will and act for His good purposes?

CONTEMPLATION ✝ REFLECT AND YIELD

How would the most important relationship in your life change if you were to think the way Christ thinks?

What mindsets or attitudes would you like to see transformed by God's grace?

PRAYER ✝ RESPOND TO GOD

Do you fully embody the mind of Christ? Open your mind to God, asking him to transform your mind to be like the mind of Jesus Christ.

INCARNATION ✝ LIVE THE WORD

The mind of Christ is not simply a way of thinking; ultimately, it is a way of living.

List three relationships in which your behavior will be affected by adopting the mind of Christ. Name one thing you will do in each relationship to place the interests of others ahead of your own.

LITTLE PEOPLE, GREAT TASKS

Listening for God through Philippians 2:19–30

SUMMARY

The Bible has many great heroes and heroines whom we admire. We revere great people such as Sarah and Abraham, Miriam and Moses, Deborah and Gideon, Mary and Peter. Yet there are multitudes of others who have done important things but are seldom remembered. These lesser-known giants also carried out great tasks for the Kingdom, but they are more often placed in footnotes than on pedestals. Where would the kingdom of God be without this legion of unsung heroes who have been faithful in little things?

In his letters Paul often makes reference to these unknown Kingdom builders. He knew that his task could never have been carried out without the work of faithful followers of

Christ who did not seek fame but simply sought to be of service. Centuries later, the kingdom of God is still advanced by women and men who are simply willing to be available wherever and whenever the Lord calls.

Are you?

SILENCE ✝ LISTEN FOR GOD

Force your busy mind to be still and spend a moment in quiet solitude. Make yourself available to God by repeating the words "Speak, Lord. I'm listening."

PREPARATION ✝ FOCUS YOUR THOUGHTS

Name three people who are not widely known but have had a significant impact on your life.

What did these people do that profoundly affected you?

Describe the character of each person in one word.

READING ✝ HEAR THE WORD

Paul made a brief digression in this letter to describe his plans to send Timothy and Epaphroditus to Philippi. Yet Paul did not completely abandon the subject under discussion; his description of both men builds nicely on his discussion of the mind of Christ.

In the introduction to Philippians, Timothy is described as the co-sender of the letter. Timothy had accompanied Paul and Silas on their second missionary journey (see Acts 16), on which Paul had established the church at Philippi. Timothy's visit would be a return to the church he had helped found.

Epaphroditus had recently brought gifts to the imprisoned Paul from the church at Philippi. Epaphroditus had then become seriously ill. Although he had recovered, the people back in Philippi had grown anxious over his illness. Therefore, Paul had determined to send Epaphroditus back home with this letter in hand.

Read aloud Philippians 2:19–30.

MEDITATION ✝ ENGAGE THE WORD

Meditate on Philippians 2:19–24

Reflect on the difference between Paul's comment that Timothy took "a genuine interest" in the Philippians' welfare and his comment that that "everyone looks out for his own interests and not those of Jesus Christ." Compare these statements to Philippians 2:4.

Why would he say he had no one else like Timothy?

Describe Timothy's character. How frequently do you encounter people like Timothy?

> It might well be that the greatest threat to human survival now confronting us is not the loss of energy or the increase of pollution, but the loss of compassion.
>
> —James C. Fenhagen,
> *Mutual Ministry*

Read the sidebar quote by James C. Fenhagen. Why is compassion such a rare commodity in our society? Do you agree with Fenhagen that the loss of compassion threatens human survival?

Do you know someone who demonstrates the same attitude that Timothy had? Describe that person.

Is Paul right in saying that most people look out for their own interests? What might cause people to be more concerned with the welfare of others?

Read the sidebar quote by Sadhu Sundar Singh. List some reasons that we tend not to reach out in selfless concern to other people.

Describe a circumstance in which you found it difficult to take an interest in the welfare of someone else.

We ought to make the best possible use of God-given opportunities and should not waste our precious time by neglect or carelessness. Many people say: there is plenty of time to do this or that; don't worry. But they do not realize that if they do not make good use of this short time, the habit formed now will be so ingrained that . . . this habit will become our second nature and we shall waste that time also.

—Sadhu Sundar Singh,
With and Without Chris

Are there people whom you find it easy to care about? Who are they, and what makes it easier to take an interest in them?

Are there people whom you find it particularly difficult to care about? Who are they, and what makes it so difficult to take an interest in them?

Meditate on Philippians 2:25–30

Paul describes Epaphroditus as his brother, fellow worker, and fellow soldier. What do each of these descriptions say about Epaphroditus's relationship to Paul?

How does Epaphroditus's willingness to risk his own life relate to the challenge Paul gave in 2:3?

Whom have you encountered on your journey who might be called your brother or sister? Your fellow worker? Your fellow soldier?

Do you know anyone whose life reflects the character traits of Epaphroditus? In what ways has that person been willing to take risks or sacrifice on behalf of others?

In which situations might you be willing to be an Epaphroditus?

In which situations would you find it difficult to be an Epaphroditus?

Read the sidebar poem by St. Teresa of Avila. Do you believe what she says? Why or why not?

CONTEMPLATION ✝
REFLECT AND YIELD

What prevents you from being a servant to other people?

How might you overcome those obstacles?

Are you ready to offer your life in service to other people if God were to open a door for you?

Christ has

No body now on earth but yours;

No hands but yours;

No feet but yours;

Yours are the eyes

Through which He looks

Compassion on the world;

Yours are the feet

With which He is to go about

Doing good;

Yours are the hands

With which He is to bless now.

—Teresa of Avila

Oratio PRAYER ✞ RESPOND TO GOD

In what ways are you serving others?

In what ways might God be calling you to serve others?

Join with a prayer partner and offer yourselves to God. Then allow Him to speak to you.

Incarnatio INCARNATION ✞ LIVE THE WORD

Name one person you will encounter this week to whom you might be of service. What will you do to make yourself useful?

MORE THAN PERFORMANCE

Listening for God through Philippians 3:1–11

SUMMARY

A performance-driven mindset dominates our culture. We often believe that "if it is to be, it is up to me." This thinking can affect the way we think about our relationship with God. It can be tempting to believe that it is the good things we do that advance our standing in God's eyes.

We might think this performance-driven approach to spirituality is a uniquely contemporary problem, but it is not. Paul confronted this way of thinking throughout his ministry. Various religious teachers infiltrated the congregations Paul had established and preached a gospel other than that based on grace. This occurred particularly in Galatia. In his letter to the Galatians, Paul exclaimed, "You foolish Galatians! Who has bewitched you?

Are you so foolish? After beginning with the Spirit, are you now trying to attain your goal by human effort?" (Galatians 3:1, 3).

From the earliest days of Christianity, the human desire to earn God's acceptance through religious or moral achievements has been a serious problem. Just as Paul challenged the earliest Christians to trust in the saving work of Christ alone, God calls us to a wholehearted reliance upon his grace. He calls us to move beyond a religion based on performance to a relationship based on faith.

SILENCE ✝ LISTEN FOR GOD

In the midst of your hurried, achievement-oriented schedule, stop! Become silent before God and reflect on His amazing grace. Now hear Him say to you, "My grace is sufficient."

PREPARATION ✝ FOCUS YOUR THOUGHTS

In what areas of your life do you feel driven to perform or achieve?

Think of a time when you felt as if your relationship with God depended upon the things you did for Him.

Lectio
READING ✝ HEAR THE WORD

With the introduction of the word *finally*, Paul makes a significant transition in his letter to the Philippians. But the letter is far from finished; Paul makes this transition only halfway through his letter.

Here Paul moves beyond his discussion of the partnership among Christians and of the mind of Christ to focus on one of his deepest, most heart-felt convictions about salvation: that it is a relationship with Christ resulting from grace alone. In this passage Paul corrects the misunderstanding of some of the Philippians.

Apparently, the Philippian church had been exposed to the teachings of a certain group of Christians demanding that non-Jewish believers be circumcised. In Paul's mind the rite of circumcision—required by law for Jews—represented an action that some might take with the motive of attempting to gain God's favor. For that reason, the demand that non-Jewish converts to Christianity be circumcised especially infuriated Paul. He firmly believed that "if righteousness could be gained through the law, Christ died for nothing" (Galatians 2:21). In his discussion, Paul makes reference to several significant terms:

Dogs: A metaphor describing the destructive nature of those persons teaching works-based salvation.

Mutilators of the flesh: Persons demanding that others be circumcised.

Confidence in the flesh: Trust in human resources or achievements.

Know: More than knowledge of facts, intimate participation in a relationship.

Righteousness: A right relationship with God and with others.

Read aloud Philippians 3:1–11.

MEDITATION ✝ ENGAGE THE WORD

Meditate on Philippians 3:1–6

Paul begins this section of his letter by warning against those persons who teach that a relationship with Christ is grounded in human ability or actions. He describes them in extremely harsh language, including the terms *dogs* and *mutilators of the flesh.*

Why would Paul take this matter so seriously? Why is this issue so important for Christian disciples to understand?

In referring to human performance in Philippians 3:4, Paul uses the word *flesh*. What other words might be used?

List the areas that Paul mentions from his religious past in which he might have placed his confidence. If Paul had been writing today, what kinds of achievements might he have named?

What areas of your own life have tended to make your feel self-confident about your relationship with God?

Why do you think it is easier for people to look at their own resources or performance as indicators of their own goodness rather than relying only on God's grace?

Do you think relying on human effort to make yourself a better person is a sensible plan? Why or why not?

Meditate on Philippians 3:7–9

Using business language, Paul says that what was once in the profit column of his life is now in the loss column. What do you think he was trying to convey?

Paul declares that every previous source of his confidence is now a loss in contrast to the "surpassing greatness of knowing Christ Jesus." In what ways is knowing Christ of greater value than human effort or achievement?

Read the sidebar quote by Charles de Foucauld. What does this statement mean for persons who place their confidence in their own resources?

You give your help, not in proportion to our merit, but to our needs. You came for the sick and not for the healthy.
    —Charles de Foucauld,
    Meditations of a Hermit

Righteousness ultimately means having a right relationship with God and others. Describe a relationship that is based on law and one based on grace. Compare and contrast the two.

Which type of relationship do you think would be easier to maintain? Which would be more satisfying? Explain your reasoning.

Read the sidebar testimony of John Wesley on page 51. In what ways does Wesley's testimony affirm Paul's teaching?

Is your relationship with God based on law or grace?

What items in your personal profit column need to be placed in the loss column?

Read the sidebar statement by Richard Rohr. Do you believe this? Why or why not?

Meditate on Philippians 3:10–11

Paul concluded this section of his letter by explaining what it means to know Christ. For Paul, this knowledge of Christ is an intimate partnership. Throughout his letter, Paul has spoken of partnerships; now he describes the details of a partnership with Jesus.

> About a quarter before nine, while he was describing the change which God works in the heart through faith in Christ, I felt my heart strangely warmed. I felt I did trust in Christ, Christ alone for salvation: And an assurance was given me, that He had taken away my sins, even mine, and saved me from the law of sin and death.
>
> —John Wesley

> Spirituality is about seeing. It's not about earning or achieving. It's about relationship rather than results or requirements.
>
> —Richard Rohr, Everything Belongs

What would a life that shares in Christ's sufferings and death be like?

What is the difference between knowing Christ and knowing about Christ? Explain your response.

Is your desire to know Christ a desire for head knowledge or for heart knowledge? In what ways would you like to see your knowledge of Christ grow?

In practical terms, what does it mean to suffer with Christ? To die with Christ?

Is it possible to experience the resurrection power of Christ without participating in His suffering and death? Why or why not?

How might suffering and dying with Christ become just another way of trusting in our own abilities or achievements?

Read the sidebar quote from Gregory of Nyssa. What does it mean that we can share a friendship with God? How do you react to that idea?

> Since the goal of the virtuous way of life is the very thing we have been seeking, it is time for you, noble friend, to be known by God and to become His friend.
>
> —Gregory of Nyssa,
> *The Life of Moses*

CONTEMPLATION ✝ REFLECT AND YIELD

In what ways would your spiritual life be changed if you were to place everything you have done in the loss column of your life and rely only on Christ for your sense of righteousness?

In what ways would your relationship with God be transformed if you were to participate in Christ's suffering, death, and resurrection?

Oratio   Prayer ✝ Respond to God

Paul makes a clear distinction between performing religious acts and having a grace-based relationship. Which method of relating to God best describes your life?

Pray silently, "I want to know You," then listen for God's direction.

Incarnatio   Incarnation ✝ Live the Word

Name two areas of your life in which Christ is calling you to suffer, die, and rise with Him. Name two actions you will take this week that will help you to know Christ more fully.

PRESSING ON AND STANDING FIRM

Listening for God through Philippians 3:12–4:1

SUMMARY

In a world that craves fast food and instant gratification, we often hear the cry: "I want it! And I want it *now*!" It is easy to import that way of thinking to spiritual life, and sometimes we look for a quick fix to spiritual problems. We want spiritual maturity, and we want it *now*!

One of the apostle's favorite metaphors for the Christian life is a race. Paul encouraged the Corinthians to "run in such a way as to get the prize" (1 Corinthians 9:24). And near the end of his ministry, he announced that he had "fought the good fight" and "finished the race" (2 Timothy 4:7). For Paul and other early Christians, the Christian life was not a destination; it was a journey.

As a follower of Christ, you, too, are called to remain focused and keep running the race—to remain faithful in your relationship with Christ.

Silencia SILENCE ✝ LISTEN FOR GOD

Allow God to speak wholeness into your life as you come silently before Him. Focus on these words of Jesus from John 14:27: "Peace I leave with you; my peace I give to you."

Praeparatio PREPARATION ✝ FOCUS YOUR THOUGHTS

Have you ever run in or watched a race?

What characteristics have you seen in successful competitors?

What potential obstacles do runners face that could prevent them from finishing? How do they avoid or overcome them?

Lectio READING ✝ HEAR THE WORD

Paul's description of the Christian life as a race directly follows his comments about sharing in the suffering, death, and resurrection of Christ. To be sure that the Philippians would not mistakenly believe that Paul was claiming to have become perfectly like Christ, Paul quickly explained that he had by no means reached the final destination. He then emphasized two important attitudes that a believer should have about the Christian life. First, because the "race" is yet unfinished, there is always room for growth—we should keep pressing on. Second, we careful not to slip back or lose ground in our spiritual journey. So the Christian life, Paul says, is lived with the simultaneous desire both to press on and to stand firm.

To describe this two-fold attitude, Paul uses several important terms:

Perfect: In this context, *perfect* means completed or finished.

Forgetting: Counting as of no value.

Prize . . . heavenward: Paul admits he has not experienced the ultimate transformation—resurrection—but he moves toward the goal.

Mature: This is the same word translated as *perfect* in verse 12. Here it describes those who are serious about making progress in the Christian life.

Read Philippians 3:12–4:1 with members of the group taking turns to read aloud one verse each.

MEDITATION ✝ ENGAGE THE WORD

Meditate on Philippians 3:12–14

Paul adamantly stated that he had not already achieved all that he had described in the previous verses and so was not yet finished, or perfect. When he wrote that he had not obtained "all this," to what do you think he referred?

Why do you think Paul was so determined to make this point?

Why do you think it was important to Paul that Jesus had first taken hold of him?

Paul said that he was forgetting what was behind. Do you think Paul was able to forget his past? Why or why not?

> What a strange thing to be new and old at the same time, to be recreated by your love and yet continue to struggle with my old self. You have freed me from the guilt and power of my own brokenness, but inner healing requires a long process of divine therapy.
>
> —Paul W. Chilcote, *Praying in the Wesleyan Spirit*

Read the sidebar quote by Paul W. Chilcote. Can you relate to what he is describing? In what ways do you struggle with your old self?

Paul also described his pressing on as straining toward what is ahead. What do you think Paul meant by "the prize"? Does this effort by Paul turn the Christian life into another performance-driven enterprise?

Read the sidebar statement by Mother Teresa. What do you believe she means by a "real living determination"? What does that type of determination look like?

Our progress in holiness depends on God and ourselves— on God's grace and on our will to be holy. We must have a real living determination to reach holiness.

—Mother Teresa, *A Gift for God*

What is the value of seeing all that lies ahead of us in our spiritual lives? How can we ensure that the statement, "I have not been made perfect," does not become an excuse for spiritual immaturity?

What in your past still needs to be forgotten? What hinders you from forgetting the past?

Could your present spiritual experience be characterized as "pressing on"? Why or why not?

What obstacles lie between you and the goal of spiritual maturity?

Read the sidebar quote by John Wesley. In light of Paul's description of the Christian life as a race, what do you believe Wesley means by "one design, one desire"?

> Always remember the essence of Christian holiness is simplicity and purity: one design, one desire: entire devotion to God.
>
> —John Wesley

Meditate on Philippians 3:15–4:1

Paraphrase this statement: "Let us live up to what we have already obtained" (3:16).

What do you think the Philippians had already obtained? What might have caused the Philippians to move backward?

Paul described certain people, saying, "Their destiny is destruction, their god is their stomach, and their glory is in their shame." What do you think their lives were probably like?

Read Mark 8:33. How does this verse relate to Paul's statement, "Their mind is on earthly things, but our citizenship is in heaven."

How does identifying oneself as a citizen of heaven promote "standing firm" on earth?

Specifically, what does it mean for you to live up to what you have already obtained? What does it mean to stand firm?

Read the sidebar quote by Joyce Rupp. Do you agree with her statement? Why or why not?

> One of the dangers of spiritual growth is that too much emphasis can be placed on "results," on how we are doing or how we are progressing.
> —Joyce Rupp,
> *The Cup of Our Life*

What people or circumstances in your life are most likely to influence you to move backward?

Read the sidebar quote by Johann Arndt. Explain what you think Arndt means when he says that love of the world can conquer the soul and the spirit.

> The love of this world, pleasure, and pride is a strong sweet wine by which the soul and the spirit are conquered.
> —Johann Arndt, *True Christianity*

Would you say that your life better reflects your citizenship on earth or in heaven? Why? Are you satisfied with your current lifestyle?

CONTEMPLATION ✝ REFLECT AND YIELD

Do you feel that you are pressing on, standing still, or moving backward in your spiritual life?

What things in your life does God invite you to forget?

Are you ready to let go of the past and move forward?

PRAYER ✝ RESPOND TO GOD

Ask God to reveal any area in which you need to stand firm or press on. Join a prayer partner in seeking God's direction for these areas of your life.

INCARNATION ✝ LIVE THE WORD

The Christian life does not consist of arriving at one spot and standing still. It is a journey. What is the next step you believe God is calling you to take on the journey to spiritual maturity? What will you do about that this week?

CHRISTIAN LIVING IN THE REAL WORLD

Listening for God through Philippians 4:2–9

SUMMARY

The Christian life is not a dream world that separates spirituality from the common affairs of life. Rather, the Christian life includes everyday relationships, ordinary concerns, and the mundane matters upon which we focus much time and energy.

Even though Paul gave much attention to matters of belief in his letters, he consistently concluded his writings with simple, practical advice on applying faith to life. Paul also frequently sent greetings to people by name along with a comment about the issues they were facing, including interpersonal conflicts, lifestyle issues, and illness or adversity. Paul never used the gospel of Christ as sedative to mask life's pain.

The gospel of Christ has ramifications for everyday life. It affects relationships, daily choices, habits, and patterns of thought. God is concerned not only with your beliefs but also with the way in which you live out those beliefs in daily life.

SILENCE ✝ LISTEN FOR GOD

God is present and active in the world. Concentrate on His presence now. Hear Him say, "I am with you."

PREPARATION ✝ FOCUS YOUR THOUGHTS

If someone wrote a song about your life, what would the title be? Why?

List three words that describe your day-to-day life.

If you could change one thing about your life, what would it be?

READING ✝ HEAR THE WORD

As Paul brought his letter to a conclusion, he exhorted the Philippians to exemplify the life of Christ. Until this point in the letter, he focused on his partnership in the gospel with the Philippians and on their shared partnership in the suffering, death, and resurrection of Christ. In his concluding remarks, Paul described in practical terms what that partnership would look like.

Paul asked that Euodia and Syntyche (two women about whom we know little) be of the same mind in the Lord. He simply wanted them to embody the mind of Christ that he had described earlier (Philippians 2). To urge this request upon the two women, Paul appeals to someone addressed as *syzygus*, which is translated *yokefellow*. Although this word may be a personal name, the term was probably chosen to emphasize the need for partnership among believers, Paul's major theme in this letter.

As you read Philippians 4:2–9, note how Paul describes the comprehensive nature of the Christian life.

Gentleness: Bearing with or giving consideration to other people.

Peace: Not an absence of turmoil but a wholeness experienced in spite of turmoil.

Guard: A military term meaning to place a sentry around.

MEDITATION ✞ ENGAGE THE WORD

Meditate on Philippians 4:2–3

Compare Paul's message in Philippians 2:5 to that of 4:2.

What is the significance of Paul's asking his "loyal yokefellow" to assist in the matter involving these two women? In what way do you think Paul expected this person to help?

Have you ever witnessed a conflict between two Christians? Name some reasons such conflicts occur.

Have you ever been a part of a conflict with another Christian? What was at the root of that conflict?

Read the sidebar quote by Hannah Whitall Smith. How would seeing Christ in a Christian with whom you have a conflict affect your attitude?

> Nothing else but this seeing God in everything will make us loving and patient with those who annoy and trouble us. . . . Christians often feel at liberty to murmur against people, when they would not dare to murmur against God.
>
> –Hannah Whitall Smith, *The Christian's Secret of a Happy Life*

Is conflict between Christians always wrong? Why or why not?

If both parties in a conflict had the "mind of Christ," what effect would that have on the conflict?

Why do people often allow conflicts to persist without working toward resolution?

Meditate on Philippians 4:4–7

Paul's call to rejoice is linked to two significant admonitions: to give consideration to others and to trust God. How do you believe these two factors relate to joy?

Why are people so often impatient with one another?

Do you think it is realistic of Paul to expect others to be completely free from worry?

Compare what Paul said here about anxiety to what Jesus said in the Sermon on the Mount (see Matthew 6:25).

What is the relationship, if any, between prayer and worry?

What is the correlation, if any, between experiencing peace and being patient with others?

How well do you do in bearing with other people? Are there specific persons with whom you are particularly impatient? Why do you find it more difficult to be patient with them?

What situations cause you to have anxiety or to worry?

What do you do to relieve your anxiety or worry?

Read the sidebar quote by John Wesley. What would it mean to pray like a child?

> Pray, just as you are led, without reasoning, in all simplicity. Be a little child, hanging on Him that loves you.
>
> —John Wesley

Why is it important to express thanks to God when making requests of Him? Why do you think people so often fail to do that?

Read the sidebar quote by Dietrich Bonhoeffer. What is your reaction to his statement?

What requests would you like to bring to God? For what blessings in your life might you thank God?

Only he who gives thanks for little things receives the big things. We prevent God from giving us the great spiritual gifts He has in store for us, because we do not give thanks for daily gifts. . . . We pray for the big things and forget to give thanks for the ordinary, small (and yet really not small) gifts. How can God entrust great things to one who will not thankfully receive from Him the little things?

—Dietrich Bonhoeffer, *Life Together*

Meditate on Philippians 4:8–9

Paul's final exhortation has to do with those things to which the Philippians should give their attention. Why is it important that Christians choose carefully what they think about?

Read the sidebar quote by Susannah Wesley, spoken to her children. Describe how this mother's advice relates to the various terms used by Paul in verse 8.

> Whatever weakens your reason, impairs the tenderness of your conscience, obscures your sense of God, or takes off the relish of spiritual things, whatever increases the authority of your body over mind, that thing for you is sin.
> —Susannah Wesley

Examine the terms used in verse 8. Name something in your life that each term could describe.

Do you focus your attention regularly upon things like these? Why or why not?

CONTEMPLATION ✝ REFLECT AND YIELD

How would your day-to-day life change if you were to demonstrate greater patience with troublesome people? If you were to consistently present your requests to God? If you were to think more intentionally about the things that become the focus of your attention?

Are you willing to make changes in these areas of your life?

Oratio PRAYER ✝ RESPOND TO GOD

Paul urges his Christian friends to apply their faith to the everyday affairs of life. How does the gospel of Christ affect your relationships? How does it affect you when facing stressful situations?

In silent prayer, ask God to guard your heart and mind with His peace.

Incarnatio INCARNATION ✝ LIVE THE WORD

Name one person with whom you might demonstrate greater patience. Name one worrisome circumstance that you will submit to God in prayer.

THE LIFE OF CONTENTMENT AND GRATITUDE

Listening for God through Philippians 4:10–23

SUMMARY

How easy it is to look at the present circumstances of life and wish for them to be different. It really is true that "the grass is always greener on the other side of the fence."

If ever there was a person who could have wished for his life to be different, it was the Apostle Paul. Throughout his ministry, Paul faced persecution, imprisonment, rejection, and sickness. Yet Paul never seemed to indulge himself in the daydream of a carefree life. While not eager to experience difficult times, Paul was able to appreciate and celebrate the grace of God experienced during hardship. By doing so, he was able to find both contentment and gratitude in spite of his difficult situation.

Like Paul, you can experience contentment as you express gratitude for God's faithful presence in your life no matter what circumstances you face.

SILENCE ✝ LISTEN FOR GOD

With both hands open, release your present circumstances to God and hear Him say, "I am always with you."

PREPARATION ✝ FOCUS YOUR THOUGHTS

If you could change one thing about your life, what would it be? Why?

If you could prevent one thing in your life from changing, what would it be? Why?

READING ✝ HEAR THE WORD

At the conclusion of his letter, Paul acknowledged a gift sent by the Philippians. While we do not know the nature of the gift, we do know that this occasion was not the first on which they assisted the apostle. Throughout Paul's ministry the Philippians had been the most generous of all the churches. Paul even referred to their generosity in one of his letters to Corinth (2 Corinthians 8:1–5; 11:9).

Paul made it clear to the Philippians that he was not wholly dependent upon their gifts. At the same time, he wanted them to realize how deeply he appreciated their assistance. Thus he expressed both contentment amid his troubling circumstances and gratitude for what they had done.

Paul uses various phrases in expressing his gratitude:

To be in need: This is the same word used in 2:8 to express the idea that Christ "humbled" himself.

Credited to your account: Paul borrowed language from the world of commerce to show that the Philippians had received dividends from the gift they had invested in Paul's ministry.

Fragrant offering: Related to Israelite offerings of thanksgiving to God.

Sacrifice: In 2:17, Paul referred to the sacrifice coming from the people's faith; their faithful gift is viewed as a sacrifice of thanksgiving.

Slowly read Philippians 4:10–23.

MEDITATION ✝ ENGAGE THE WORD

While expressing gratitude to the Philippians for their gift, Paul emphasized that even without the gift, he was content. What events in Paul's life that might have helped to teach him the lesson of contentment?

How would you define *contentment*? Is there a difference between contentment and happiness? Why or why not?

Paul says he has learned the secret in being content in any and every situation. What do you believe this secret is?

Do you think it is possible to be content in all situations of life? Why or why not?

How is Paul's declaration that he can do all things through Christ who gives him strength related to the contentment he has discovered?

Compare what Paul wrote here with his words in 2 Corinthians 12:7–10. What similarities or differences do you see in these passages?

Name a circumstance or situation in your life that caused you to feel discontent. If Paul were to give you advice about that situation, what do you think he might say?

Read the sidebar quote by William Shakespeare. How does remembering God's past faithfulness make an impact upon your present situation?

> God's goodness hath been great to thee; Let never day or night unhallowed pass, But still remember what the Lord hath done.
>
> —William Shakespeare

Do you believe that you, too, can do all things through Him who gives you strength? Why or why not?

Meditate on Philippians 4:15-23

Paul listed the times in which the Philippians had shared in his adversities. What do you think Paul meant by saying that they "shared" his troubles?

Why do you think the generous actions of the Philippians made such a profound impact upon Paul?

Read the sidebar quote from Henri Nouwen, Donald McNeill, and Doulgas Morrison on page 78. Why is it easier to give gifts or money from a distance than to get close to people in need?

What did Paul mean when he wrote that rather than looking for a gift, he was looking for what the Philippians had credited to their account by giving to him? In what ways does giving a gift benefit the giver?

Why do you think Paul called the service of the Philippians a pleasing sacrifice to God when it was Paul that they served? Read Micah 6:6–8 and compare that prophet's words with Paul's statements to the Philippians. In what ways are they similar? Are there any differences?

> It is not bending toward the underprivileged from a privileged position; it is not a reaching out from on high to those who are less fortunate below; it is not a gesture of sympathy or pity for those who fail to make it in the upward pull. On the contrary, compassion means going directly to those people and places where suffering is most acute and building a home there.
>
> –Henri Nouwen,
> Donald McNeill,
> Douglas Morrison, *Compassion*

In verse 19 Paul suddenly shifted the focus away from himself, saying, "My God will meet all your needs." Why might Paul have made this shift?

What do you think Paul meant by "all your needs"? What things do you need? What things do you long for but don't truly need?

Read the words from the Shaker song in the sidebar. How does the call to simplicity help define the genuine needs of our lives? Is there a correlation between practicing simplicity and experiencing contentment? If so, what?

> 'Tis the gift to be simple, 'tis the gift to be free,
>
> 'tis the gift to come down where we ought to be,
>
> And when we find ourselves in the place just right,
>
> 'twill be in the valley of love and delight.
>
> —Eighteenth Century Shaker Song

Describe a time when someone shared in your adversity or you shared in someone else's. What impact did this sharing have upon you?

Do you struggle to accept the idea that God will meet all of your needs "according to His glorious riches in Christ Jesus"? If so, why? What might make it easier for you to accept that belief?

CONTEMPLATION ✝ REFLECT AND YIELD

How would your life be different if you could learn to be content in every situation?

In what areas of your life do you most need the assurance that you can do all things through God's strength?

PRAYER ✝ RESPOND TO GOD

Choose a prayer partner. As you pray together, ask God to make His strength real in your lives.

After praying, speak these words of affirmation to one another: "My God will meet all your needs according to His glorious riches in Christ."

INCARNATION ✝ LIVE THE WORD

Name a situation that you will likely face this week in which you must depend completely upon God's strength. Then finish the sentence: The secret to experiencing contentment in my life this week is to . . . .